THE DISHWASHERS

Morris Panych

Talonbooks
Vancouver

Talonbooks
P.O. Box 2076, Vancouver, British Columbia, Canada V6B 3S3
www.talonbooks.com

Typeset in New Baskerville and printed and bound in Canada.

Second Printing: 2008

The publisher gratefully acknowledges the financial support of the Canada Council for the Arts; the Government of Canada through the Book Publishing Industry Development Program; and the Province of British Columbia through the British Columbia Arts Council for our publishing activities.

Library and Archives Canada Cataloguing in Publication

Panych, Morris
    The dishwashers / Morris Panych.

A play.
ISBN 0-88922-524-9

    I. Title.

PS8581.A65D48 2005   C812'.54   C2005-902476-3

ISBN-13: 978-0-88922-524-4

The Dishwashers premiered on February 17, 2005 at the Arts Club Theatre in Vancouver, British Columbia, with the following cast and crew:

DRESSLER . . . . Stephen E. Miller
EMMETT . . . . Ted Cole
MOSS . . . . Shawn Macdonald
BURROUGHS . . . . Toby Berner

Director: Morris Panych
Set Design: Ken MacDonald
Lighting Design: Gerald King
Costume Design: Nancy Bryant
Sound Design: Darren W. Hales
Stage Manager: Caryn Fehr
Assistant Stage Manager: Anne Taylor

AUTHOR'S NOTE

So often with plays that have – for lack of a better description – an absurdist bent, theatre artists can and will take liberties with both their dialogue and their stage directions that they might not otherwise attempt. Absurd and comic situations such as those often found in my plays should not give license to producers, actors and directors to bend reality all out of shape with overacting and silly direction. In my mind, the absurdities of the situations I have created are real, the people involved in them are real, and the outcome has high stakes for the characters involved in the world the drama creates. In *The Dishwashers,* I have created a situation that cannot play without the complete believability and integrity of all of the elements of the production: acting, directing, design. Sometimes, with the set for example, Ken MacDonald and I will try to convey a dreamlike sense of reality that should not be confused with non-reality. A dream, when you are in it, is real; sometimes frightening, sometimes alarming, sometimes funny, but the stakes for you in its "reality" are always high, and the existential outcome of its events is always vital. If you have ever woken from a nightmare, screaming, or ever found yourself laughing out loud in your sleep, you will know how deeply real and truthful a dream can appear to be. So it should be with any production of this play.

The Dishwashers is dedicated to my father, Peter Panych; a hard-working and decent man – one of millions, quietly, unobtrusively, keeping the wheels turning.

Morris Panych
August 2005

ACT ONE

Scene One

In the cellar of a restaurant; piles of dishes impressively high; to one side a dumbwaiter, bringing more dishes. Other washing equipment; sprayers, scrub brushes, etc. Two men are standing more or less in the middle of the room. DRESSLER, the older and heftier of the two, arm around the younger man's shoulder, shows EMMETT the ropes.

DRESSLER

I just hope you got the right stuff for this.

EMMETT

Why – why do you say that?

DRESSLER

I don't know. I just hope you do. I look at your hands and I wonder. That's all.

EMMETT considers his hands.

EMMETT

Manual labour isn't really my –

DRESSLER

You look more like – your what?

EMMETT

– thing.

DRESSLER

– more like busboy material to me. Why'd they send you down here, I have to ask myself.

EMMETT

I prefer this, actually.

DRESSLER

You don't say.

EMMETT

There's a – certain degree of – what's the word? –

DRESSLER

I don't know.

EMMETT

– anonymity.

DRESSLER

You got that right. We had a guy down here once, went completely out of his mind. You know what he was doing – he was hiding from the truth.

Beat. They study one another.

EMMETT

R-ight.

DRESSLER

Know what this is?

EMMETT

A hose?

DRESSLER

That's your hot sprayer. See? That's for spackle. Know what I'm talking about? Stuff that hardens on the plate. Tomato coulis, béchamel, pesto –

you get the picture. That's your Achilles' tendon of dishwashing, that. Look at that. I don't give a damn about your modern technology; that isn't coming off in *any* machine. No way. Feel that. Don't be afraid of it – feel it. Go on.

EMMETT

Mm.

DRESSLER

Parmesan. Get to know your enemy.

Another beat as they eye each other.

It's teamwork down here.

EMMETT

Gotcha.

DRESSLER

Is that a tattoo?

EMMETT

No.

DRESSLER

Looks like a tattoo.

EMMETT

Just the address. I didn't have a –

DRESSLER

Uh, huh.

EMMETT

– piece of paper.

DRESSLER

Is there a story?

EMMETT

Not – that I can – think of.

DRESSLER

I'd like to talk for a moment about trust, if I may. I'm going to roll up my sleeves here. What's your name again?

EMMETT

Emmett.

DRESSLER

Wrong. It's "new guy." Got that?

EMMETT

OK.

DRESSLER

You'll know you've gained my trust, finally, when I start using your real name. That'll be a moment, between us. You know? A rite of passage.

EMMETT

I see.

DRESSLER

I'll look over at you one day, and I'll just – right out of the blue – I'll say "hey" – uh – what's the name, sorry?

EMMETT

Emmett.

DRESSLER

That's it. I'll look over at you, with a little half-smile, and I'll say "Hey, Emmett."

Beat.

That'll be a moment.

EMMETT
Right.

DRESSLER
But you have to earn that.

EMMETT
Right.

Beat.

How?

DRESSLER
Eh?

EMMETT
How do I earn that?

DRESSLER
Trust.

EMMETT
OK.

DRESSLER
What do you see all around you?

EMMETT
Dishes?

DRESSLER
Try to look at the bigger picture.

Beat.

EMMETT

Endless dishes.

DRESSLER

I'll tell you what I see. Responsibility. Got that? You know what happens if one dirty dish gets through, new guy? We all go down. You think Mr. and Mrs. Fancy Pants, in all their best finery, sitting up there – you think when they tuck into that rocket salad, with the lemon-sage dressing and those little herbed croutons, and they look down to encounter an encrusted speck of *basil* on the rim of the plate – you think they care if it's you or me who let that happen? We're the people they don't ever want to know about. Ever. We're like the foundations of this very building. *Unseen reliability*. Got that? What?

EMMETT

Huh?

DRESSLER

Good. You only think about us when the whole operation starts to fall apart. And we don't want that to happen. We work together as a team, here, to make sure it doesn't. You like your anonymity? You got it. What's wrong? What is it?

EMMETT

These pants look kind of –

DRESSLER

Do they?

EMMETT

Do you have another – ?

DRESSLER

No.

Beat.

The guy before was a – I guess the technical term is dwarf.

EMMETT

What happened to him?

DRESSLER

He never grew?

EMMETT

Here, I mean.

DRESSLER

What do you think? He was a fuck-up.

EMMETT

You have higher standards?

DRESSLER

We don't talk about it.

EMMETT

OK.

DRESSLER

Maybe you could take down the hem a little.

EMMETT

If there *was* any, that would be – yeah.

DRESSLER

There's always a solution. If the pants don't fit you, then maybe you have to fit the pants. Know what I mean?

EMMETT
No.

DRESSLER
Good. What?

EMMETT
Huh?

DRESSLER
My name is Dressler. That's all you need to know about me for the time being. I don't like to divulge too much at once.

EMMETT
No.

DRESSLER
I had a testicle removed. For example. That might be something I don't want out in the open.

EMMETT
Not a testicle, no.

DRESSLER
It was a clerical error.

EMMETT
Ouch.

DRESSLER
These things happen.

EMMETT
They do?

DRESSLER

Where are *you* from? Don't answer that. It's a rhetorical question. Rhetorical? Know what that is? Hospitals. You don't know what goes on.

EMMETT

Gee.

DRESSLER

Things happen. You go in with a hernia – it's anybody's guess. But you make it work. You know where a guy's nuts are?

Beat.

EMMETT

You want me to answer that?

DRESSLER

(*indicating*) They're up here.

EMMETT

Sure.

DRESSLER

Wait a minute. You're not patronizing me, are you? Just curious.

EMMETT

No.

DRESSLER

OK. Just curious. Because, listen. I'm twice the man you are, and then some. Don't – overly concern yourself with my balls.

Showing his big flabby stomach.

Look at this, new guy. Can you believe the shape I'm in? Look.

EMMETT

I –

DRESSLER

Is that beautiful or what? Do you see any fat on me? Whatsoever?

Beat.

EMMETT

Is this a trick question?

DRESSLER

You seem a little lacking in confidence, if you don't mind my saying. Maybe it's your – I don't know – lack of a formal education. Could that be it?

EMMETT

I have a degree. Actually.

DRESSLER

That'll come in quite handy. I mean that sincerely. What was your special field of study?

EMMETT

English.

DRESSLER

English. OK.

EMMETT

Not a whole degree.

DRESSLER

Uh, huh.

EMMETT

I decided to go out and make some money. So I – went out and made some money. A considerable amount of it.

DRESSLER

Is that so?

EMMETT

Then I – yeah, lost a considerable amount; considerable being – all of it. Do we have to talk about this?

DRESSLER

We don't have to talk about it.

EMMETT

I've had a run of bad luck.

DRESSLER

And now your luck is changing for the better.

Beat.

EMMETT

Right.

DRESSLER

You don't seem like a foreigner at all, if I may say so.

EMMETT

No?

DRESSLER

No.

EMMETT

I'm not.

DRESSLER

Interesting.

EMMETT

Is it?

DRESSLER

Not really. I'm only saying because considering how you never actually finished your English degree, per se, you speak it fairly well.

Beat.

EMMETT

Thank you.

DRESSLER

Try not to get a swelled head, though. A guy doesn't want to get too big for his britches down here.

EMMETT looks at his pants.

EMMETT

And yet –

DRESSLER

Eh?

EMMETT

Huh?

DRESSLER

What?

EMMETT

Sorry?

DRESSLER

On the other hand, you need to stay sharp and ahead of the game. You can crumble in a place like this. Crumble, and disintegrate. Like those, uh, you know, what are they called?

EMMETT

I don't –

DRESSLER

Huh?

EMMETT

What are what called?

DRESSLER

I found this potato once, in the back of my cupboard, and I guess it must have been there for months. Sure. It looked like a potato, on the outside, but when I went to pick it up, it completely fell apart in my hands. Dust. I think that's a lesson for all of us. Don't you?

EMMETT

A potato.

DRESSLER

About neglect. Atrophy. Know what that is, Mr. I-Can-Speak-English? Atrophy? My secret, of course. I work out. Look at this bicep. It's important to stay in shape. Feel that.

EMMETT

Holy – Dinah.

Beat.

DRESSLER

It's not appropriate to say "Holy Dinah" in this country. Just so you know, it makes you sound like a – you know?

EMMETT

People don't usually show me their biceps.

DRESSLER

No?

EMMETT

I have a hard time with muscles and – spontaneity.

DRESSLER

Would you say that you have a healthy sexual appetite towards women at all?

EMMETT

Uh –

DRESSLER

Just asking. It's your prerogative. Would you characterize yourself as ambiguous, then?

EMMETT

You don't need to know this. Do you need to know this?

DRESSLER

No.

EMMETT

I'm engaged. Is that – ?

DRESSLER

Here or back in the old country?

EMMETT

What?

DRESSLER

I would like to draw your attention, now, to this area over here. This is your locker, of course. Belonged to your diminutive predecessor. You can take down the nudie pictures if they disturb you in any way.

EMMETT

Dwarves, are they?

DRESSLER

I beg your pardon?

EMMETT

I only figured since he was so – you said he was a dwarf.

DRESSLER

He never thought of himself in that way. As far as he was concerned, he was a large person trapped inside a small person's body. Perhaps we should all take note of that.

EMMETT

Sure.

DRESSLER

Washroom.

EMMETT

Right.

DRESSLER

Sanitation; the cornerstone of good restaurant management. Pubic hair in a lobster bisque is just the sort of thing we want to avoid.

EMMETT

Mm.

DRESSLER

This here is the time sheet. They never bother changing the names, of course. People come and go. They're much too busy up there. Much. Too. Busy. You're "Koslowski," for the purposes of the time sheet. That's you. See? I'm "Wong."

They study the sheet for a beat.

Engaged?

EMMETT

What? Yes.

DRESSLER

You don't say. This here is where notices get posted. For example, a staff meeting might get posted here.

EMMETT

How often are those?

DRESSLER

What?

EMMETT

Staff meetings?

DRESSLER

Never. But why do you ask? I find that interesting.

EMMETT

Do you?

DRESSLER

No. This is the lunch area here. Meals, as you know, are provided by the restaurant. We don't eat what the people upstairs eat; if that's what you're driving at.

EMMETT

I'm not driving at –

DRESSLER

Eh?

EMMETT

What?

A horrid fit of coughing can be heard. From the top of the stairs, a very old man makes his way down; stopping occasionally for a breather. This is MOSS, a hundred-year-old, chain-smoking, crab-ass.

DRESSLER

Oh, Jesus.

EMMETT

Who is it?

DRESSLER

Act natural. This here is my chair. The whole area, here, as you can see, has been carefully marked off for my newspaper. I may not actually be reading a newspaper at the time, but don't let that lead you into a false sense of space at all. At any time, without warning, I could decide to take out a newspaper and read it. On-the-spur-of-the-moment type thing. It's called *latitude*, is what it's called. Eventually, you may work your way up to this kind of latitude, but it won't be in the short term.

MOSS lands at the bottom of the stairs. DRESSLER makes a point of ignoring him, but EMMETT can't help looking. MOSS stands, breathing heavily. He stares hard at EMMETT for a long moment; then a look to DRESSLER.

DRESSLER

(*to MOSS*) Don't ask me.

MOSS

You must be kidding.

DRESSLER

He's engaged, apparently.

MOSS

Him?

MOSS shuffles over to the washroom and shuts the door, as both EMMETT and DRESSLER watch in silence.

A beat.

DRESSLER

That's Moss.

EMMETT

Right.

DRESSLER

The guy is riddled with cancer.

EMMETT

That's –

DRESSLER

It's one of his better qualities; but hey, he's a human being.

As he exits with EMMETT following.

What's the word for "terminal" where you come from?

EMMETT

Terminal.

DRESSLER

That's handy. Those are potatoes. Follow me.

They go out the back way. A beat. MOSS appears in the bathroom doorway; slowly he shuts it again. Blackout. Music; a cacophony of steam and dishes.

Scene Two

Coffee break. DRESSLER sits at one end reading a paper, carefully turning the pages so that they fit within his parameters. MOSS sits at the other end, smoking and staring at the wall.

DRESSLER

I've been thinking about crème brûlée.

He turns a page.

Why is there such a deep inner satisfaction in cracking through a hard surface? Is it the softness beneath? The touching notion that if we really search for it, we will find the good in everything; if not the good, at least the vulnerable; the underbelly of the beast. That life's hardness is only part of the story? My father was a miserable fucking bastard. Beat me senseless, on occasion. But a rousing chorus of "My Hero" from *The Chocolate Soldier* could always bring a tear to his eye. Oh, look. Toilet paper's on sale. And they say it's all bad news.

MOSS

Don't let go of the rope!

DRESSLER

What?

MOSS

Eh?

DRESSLER

Wake up. You're daydreaming.

MOSS

I'm not.

DRESSLER

You are.

MOSS

My mind is as sharp as a tack.

DRESSLER

Is that right.

MOSS

Just look at this concentration.

He focuses intently, putting himself into a trance.

DRESSLER

Moss.

MOSS
Eh?

DRESSLER
You dozed off there.

MOSS
I was contemplating.

DRESSLER
What do you have to contemplate?

MOSS
My own redundancy.

DRESSLER
Cheer up for fuck's sake.

MOSS
What if they let me go? It happens. A guy doesn't hold up his end.

DRESSLER
They'd never do that.

MOSS
This is a two-man operation. Now there's three. You think I can't add and subtract?

DRESSLER
We've had three men before. There was the dwarf, and the Venezuelan with the temper before him, the guy with the sleepy eye who never spoke, that Vietnamese transsexual.

MOSS
She wasn't anything of the kind. Just a nice girl with muscles.

DRESSLER

Downsizing. Upsizing. They can't make up their fucking minds.

Continues reading.

Whenever he gets the slightest opportunity, the guy runs and locks himself in the john. Have you noticed?

MOSS

They come over here, and they don't like anybody, these immigrants. Haven't we got enough people in this country that don't like anybody?

DRESSLER

He's not what you'd call affable.

MOSS

Why go back to a third man? It doesn't make economic sense.

DRESSLER

How should I know? They don't appraise me of every little piss-ass detail. As with all things managerial, it has to do with "restructuring."

MOSS

And here's another thing; why haven't I been paid this week?

DRESSLER

You've been paid.

MOSS

Have I?

DRESSLER

You tend to forget these things.

MOSS

Forget what things?

DRESSLER

Sometimes, life repeats itself with such blinding regularity that events appear not to have happened at all. There's a term for it if I'm not mistaken.

MOSS

There is?

DRESSLER

I believe it's called "the fog of recognition."

MOSS

You made that up.

DRESSLER

Take, for example, a fork. Does anyone question four tines? We don't have the time or the inclination, and so it all gets folded into the brown gravy of inevitability.

MOSS

Do you have any idea how full of shit you are?

DRESSLER

You've gone and bought something and don't remember. It wouldn't be the first time.

MOSS

No?

DRESSLER

Aren't you the proud owner of a tortoise?

MOSS

I had a chance to buy half this town, once.

DRESSLER

Don't go on about that property again; Christ.

MOSS

No; I bought the sedan instead. That was the beginning of the end.

DRESSLER

You had no vision.

MOSS

I thought it would get me somewhere.

DRESSLER

It got you here.

MOSS

Rusted-out heap of shit.

DRESSLER

Whatever happened to that famous old car of yours? I can't remember.

MOSS

We left it by the side of the road, George.

DRESSLER

Who?

MOSS

Eh?

DRESSLER

Lately you've been calling me George.

MOSS

I haven't.

DRESSLER

Must've been before my time.

MOSS

What?

DRESSLER

Eh?

EMMETT comes out of the washroom in his ill-fitted whites, carrying the newspaper.

Here he is, Moss.

MOSS

Who?

DRESSLER

Moss thinks you're hiding from us on your breaks in there. Avoiding the pleasure of our company.

EMMETT

I'm not feeling well.

DRESSLER

Exactly. I told the old man, "if it's his bowels, best to keep our noses out of it."

Break bell. The break is over. MOSS goes to his station and begins scraping food off of plates. Occasionally, he picks out interesting bits of scrap and eats them. Momentarily, the other two join him at the buspans.

DRESSLER

Nevertheless, a discussion is underway about your attitude here. Are those the want ads?

EMMETT
Attitude?

DRESSLER
There's an opinion going around that you think of yourself as superior.

EMMETT
It's inadvertent.

DRESSLER
I hope you don't consider yourself too grand for this line of work.

EMMETT
I'm getting used to it. The dishes part is a little hard to take, but other than that –

DRESSLER
You think of this as a manual labour. That's your problem, new guy. Don't think of it as manual labour.

EMMETT
It's just that it's – so much *like* manual labour.

DRESSLER
It is, isn't it? When you look at it from a certain angle, it is. Just an interminable stack of mind-numbing drudgery.

MOSS
Try bricklaying.

EMMETT
No thank you.

MOSS

Brick, mortar, brick, mortar, brick, mortar, brick, lunch, mortar, brick, mortar –

DRESSLER

I think we get the picture, Moss. A man of your imagination and intellect, new guy, ought to be able to adapt his thinking. You know what I'd do in this situation?

EMMETT

You are in this situation.

DRESSLER

Mind over matter. I don't see a stack of plates in front of me. I see an Olympic stadium with a hundred thousand spectators; I see judges waiting with their scores; one set of scores for cleanliness, the other for sheer style of execution. Don't see what's in front of you. If people saw what was in front of them, they'd self-annihilate.

EMMETT

All the positive thinking in the world won't make a dirty dish clean.

DRESSLER

Set goals for yourself.

EMMETT

I have is the problem.

DRESSLER

When I say goals, I don't necessarily mean unachievable ones. Look at Moss. Sets his heights too high; always has.

MOSS

I'd like to see the world from outer space before I die; is that so much to ask?

DRESSLER

Not if you were a cosmonaut monkey.

MOSS

I'm not.

DRESSLER

Only by the slimmest of margins. One dish at a time, new guy; that's the way to do it. You can't go wrong. Dump this, while you're up.

Beat.

EMMETT

I need the dumpster key.

DRESSLER

Just leave it on top.

EMMETT

It's meat; the rats get it.

DRESSLER

On top.

EMMETT grabs a large green garbage bag and exits around the corner. They watch him go.

Try to remember; we were young once.

MOSS

Working our way up.

Beat.

Except for the "up" part.

DRESSLER

We wanted things. We dreamed. And then we found out.

MOSS

Right. What?

DRESSLER

Eh?

MOSS

What did we find out?

DRESSLER

You know. The pointlessness of it all. The mad dash to the finish line.

MOSS

Why can't I win the lottery before I die? I've been so loyal to those numbers.

DRESSLER

What would you do with all that money? Think if you were a millionaire, Moss. You might never want your life to end. As it is now, you have so little to relinquish. I figure the happiest creature on earth is some cockroach; crawling around in dark filthy corners; unattractive and unwanted. When he's finally stepped on, imagine how relieved he must be to no longer exist.

They think.

MOSS

I'd buy this restaurant and burn it to the ground.

EMMETT returns.

EMMETT

That meat was perfectly good.

DRESSLER

Depends what you mean by perfectly good. Before you resume, I'd like to raise the issue of loading, if I may.

EMMETT

It's an issue?

DRESSLER

It certainly can be. We can't be redoing your work here because of incorrect loading procedures.

MOSS

Keep up your end, pal.

DRESSLER

We run out of salad plates, finished, game's up.

MOSS

It's over.

DRESSLER

Timing is all that matters up there. You think it's just a question of bringing people their food? Think again. Up there, new guy, up there, is a subtle arrangement of chaos. You've got an oasis of calm surrounded by a sandstorm, is what you've got. At the centre, of course, sits the diner. He or she, like a sultan, if I may carry the desert metaphor a little further, relaxed and undisturbed by what engulfs them. Nothing must interfere with that. Nothing. For them, time evaporates, conversations flow, ideas meld like candle wax, into one another, agreements are made, marriages proposed; you can't have one of these people looking at their watch, suddenly, and thinking "where the fuck's my appetizer?" It doesn't work. You can't have the customer suddenly become aware of what's really going on. That a bunch of guys in cheap tuxedos are standing around, looking at their own asses in the mirror? That, *wait a minute*, figs don't really go with organ meat of any kind? That they're drinking fifty-year-old Chateau What-Have-You like tap water? No. In the truest sense, you want the customer to leave here, not even realizing they've been; to float out that revolving door, and into the street, like the whole thing was a beautiful epicurean dream.

MOSS
A mirage.

DRESSLER
At least a width of a finger separates the plates at all times. Got that? If a plate touches another plate, forget it. Glassware is washed in a separate load; that goes without saying. To prevent filminess, we use a different soap-to-water ratio. But don't let modern mechanization lull you into a false sense of security. You've got to remain vigilant about it. Always. Jesus; I've seen a brandy snifter come out of here that would drain the blood from your neck.

MOSS
I've seen worse.

DRESSLER
What we do down here has wider implications.

MOSS
Affects the whole operation.

DRESSLER

I don't think integral would be an exaggeration.

EMMETT

No?

DRESSLER

Think of the look on chef's face, as he plates the food up there. The careful arrangement of ideas, set upon this dish, the balance; the presentation. It starts with us, down here, with us, new guy. We're the vanguard; the front line.

MOSS

Without us, they'd be picking fingerling potatoes off their laps, the bastards.

EMMETT

I used to be one of those bastards.

DRESSLER

You ate in this restaurant?

EMMETT

Ironic, but yes.

MOSS

Yes.

EMMETT

Seems like a lifetime ago.

DRESSLER

Then you understand only too well what's at stake here.

EMMETT

I hate to tell you, but I never noticed the dishes. Not once.

DRESSLER

Exactly.

Blackout.

Scene Three

The men are wearing little red Christmas hats, MOSS is working at the sink. EMMETT watches with a mixture of awe and disdain. For a while there is nothing but the sound of dishes being scraped and stacked.

EMMETT

Do you ever think about anything while you work, Moss? What do you think about?

MOSS continues, unfazed.

Politics?

MOSS

No.

EMMETT

Art? Pornography? Do you ever think about naked women, when you're slipping your hand around in the grease traps?

MOSS

That's obscene.

EMMETT

Of course it's obscene. That's the point. Anything to take your mind off the work. Isn't that the idea? Or do you ponder bigger questions? Surely to God you have to ponder something. Surely to God, in the absence of any physical escape from here, the mind, at least, is an open door.

MOSS

I used to think about things all the time. Look where it got me.

EMMETT

Ever think about retiring?

MOSS

No.

EMMETT

No.

MOSS

What would I do?

EMMETT

Travel?

MOSS

Where?

EMMETT

Haven't you ever wanted to go anywhere?

MOSS

Why do you want me to go somewhere?

EMMETT

I'm only saying the time may come, when you have finally petrified yourself into a hardened stump of oldness so old that archeologists are brought in to chip the salad plate out of your hand – that you may decide, gee, maybe I've been here long enough. Maybe I should go somewhere else.

MOSS

It'll never happen. And anyway, I haven't got any money.

EMMETT

Right.

MOSS

Somebody's stealing it.

EMMETT

They are, are they.

MOSS

Dressler.

EMMETT

Dressler?

MOSS

You don't believe me.

EMMETT

I don't know.

MOSS

I had an opportunity to buy some property, once. Why didn't I? No, I was drawn to the glamour of the restaurant world.

EMMETT

Right.

MOSS

Before I washed dishes, I washed cars.

EMMETT

Fantastic.

MOSS

Those were the days, George. Sunshine, bubbles.

EMMETT

George?

MOSS

Eh?

DRESSLER enters from above.

DRESSLER

Well – I've been upstairs.

EMMETT

And?

DRESSLER

One day you should go up there. You really should. When the opportunity is right. It might reaffirm your faith in the place, to see it running like – well, I know this is a cliché, but like a Swiss ship.

EMMETT

So do we get off early?

DRESSLER

The question didn't arise. As such.

EMMETT

What do you mean the question didn't arise?

DRESSLER

As such, no.

EMMETT

Correct me if I'm wrong, but isn't that why you went up there in the first place?

DRESSLER
These aren't your everyday employers.

EMMETT
No?

DRESSLER
It needs to come up in the conversation; naturally. They're people of incredibly subtle style. They can get a hundred dollars out of you for a chicken dinner.

EMMETT
It's Christmas Eve. I have plans.

DRESSLER
What sort of plans?

EMMETT
I have a date, if you must know. A date.

DRESSLER
The fiancée?

EMMETT
Maybe.

MOSS
She still around?

EMMETT
Yes, she's still around.

DRESSLER
Don't worry. We can cover for you.

EMMETT
Thank you.

DRESSLER

But you're wasting your time. Women don't like dishwashers.

EMMETT

No?

DRESSLER

Generally speaking, they have bigger plans for us.

EMMETT

I've had no complaints, so far.

DRESSLER

She doesn't know what you do, then, does she? She hasn't been appraised of your current social status.

EMMETT

Of course she has. No, she hasn't. Her family wouldn't approve; end of story. Would you excuse me?

DRESSLER

I'm not standing in your way.

EMMETT

You are standing in my way.

DRESSLER

Step around me.

EMMETT

Why should I?

MOSS

Why shouldn't you?

EMMETT

Alright.

He steps around DRESSLER.

DRESSLER

See that, Moss. Compromises himself. Doesn't stand his ground. Is it any wonder he never made it in the corporate world?

EMMETT

On the contrary, I did make it, Dressler. I made quite a lot of it, in fact.

MOSS

Then you lost it.

DRESSLER

Tragic.

EMMETT

Why am I being confronted here? What is this?

DRESSLER

You see your job here as a failure. This is the success part. Isn't that right, Moss?

MOSS

The acme.

EMMETT

I don't see it as a failure. I see it – yes, as a failure. I see it – yes. You're right about that. I don't see this as success. Is this a success? Hm. Let's see. I used to eat in this restaurant, and now I wash dishes in it. What would you call that?

DRESSLER

You lost everything, in your opinion.

EMMETT

That's right. I lost everything. Not in my opinion. In the bank's opinion.

DRESSLER

But what did you really have?

EMMETT

What did I *have*? I had money, *money*; I had a big beautiful apartment, overlooking the water, Dressler. Not just a little water, a *lot* of water. What am I overlooking, now? Nothing; because the room I'm living in – did I say room? – doesn't have a window. It's one thing, Dressler, to never have had anything. But it's quite another to have had it all, and watch it slip through your fingers. Paradise Lost; that's what it is. Who do you think is happier in life? The blind man who used to see, or the blind man who never saw at all?

MOSS

The retarded man who collects all the bottles.

EMMETT

We're not talking about a retarded man who collects bottles. Are we talking about a retarded man who collects bottles?

MOSS

He's the happiest man I've ever seen.

DRESSLER

Of course he is; he's retarded.

EMMETT

I was talking about a blind man. I was talking about the loss of something. About how a man feels when everything he is, the very foundation of his being, is swept away. Not even swept away; that, he would be able to see. No. He just wakes up one morning to find it all gone; his entire worth. Like that. Evaporated into the air like – like not a real thing, but an idea; something that existed only as a mathematical possibility. And then someone changed the equation. Numbers on a chalkboard, erased. "Oops. Sorry, Emmett. Sorry. Oh, well. It's only money." No. It isn't. It's *my* money! See. Pronoun. Missing. That's me. Missing. Gone.

DRESSLER

You're hardly gone. You're here.

A beat. EMMETT goes to change.

Just us, then.

They go back to work.

MOSS

How can I retire?

DRESSLER

Who's retiring?

MOSS

I don't know. Ask him.

DRESSLER

No one's retiring. What would you do?

MOSS

Travel, he says.

DRESSLER

Travel. Look at you.

MOSS

Look at me.

DRESSLER

You're not going anywhere.

MOSS

What would I do when I got there?

DRESSLER

You'd long to be back. I went on a holiday, once. Not so much a holiday as a train derailment. There was another time, too. Some lake, somewhere. Nearly went out of my mind. Children, dogs, nothing to do. So I constructed in my mind a brilliant novel. Well, really a novella. A mystery. It starts like this: "Elsewhere, things were quiet; but here along the water, the sound of a body washing up against the pier." I felt that beginning a story with the word "elsewhere" would have a kind of subtly unhinging effect on the reader. Not to mention the complete absence of a verb. "Where's the verb?" You see? Opening sentence, already a mystery.

MOSS

Spare time is the bane of my existence.

DRESSLER

Is it?

MOSS

Sunday is the most pointless day of the week.

DRESSLER

I can't agree.

MOSS

For one thing, the "sun" part of it is completely misleading.

DRESSLER

I think Wednesday has got it all over Sunday for pointlessness. First off, you've got that extra *d* nobody wants.

MOSS

True.

DRESSLER

And look where it is; directly between Tuesday and Thursday. Could there be a more futile situation?

EMMETT

(*popping his head around the corner*) He could enjoy the rest of his life is the point I was trying to make.

MOSS

(*as he goes off to the john*) What if I'm enjoying not enjoying it?

EMMETT

Sorry I brought it up.

DRESSLER

Don't bring it up again.

EMMETT

Look at him. He can hardly make his way across the room.

DRESSLER gets close; deliberate.

DRESSLER

You want to destroy the man?

EMMETT

He's already destroyed.

DRESSLER

There'll be no more talk about retirement. Rest of his life? A turkey at a Christmas market has better chances.

EMMETT

Fine. But he's old and he's sick.

DRESSLER

Which is why he's been replaced.

EMMETT

Is that – ? Uh, huh. By who?

DRESSLER

You. Didn't I ever mention that? Oh. He's been replaced by you.

EMMETT

Wait a minute. Since when?

DRESSLER

Since the day you started. Merry Christmas.

Blackout.

Scene Four

New Year's Eve. Champagne bottles half full.

DRESSLER

What a time they're having up there.

Long silence as the revelry continues above them.

Look at this. Fois gras. When was the last time you saw this in such *proliferation*? If this isn't the economy trickling down, I don't know what is.

MOSS

I prefer the whole roasted moulard to this fucking Gewurztraminer-poached.

DRESSLER

Now, this is the kind of plate I like to see. A filet mignon with only one little bite out of it, and a cigar stuck into the smashed blue potatoes. Beautiful. What an extraordinary little monument to overindulgence. These are people who know how to throw their money around.

EMMETT

It never occurred to me how disgusting this was.

DRESSLER

You're jealous, that's all.

EMMETT

Here's the thing; I'm not, actually. If that's the kind of person I was, this wasteful, gluttonous, boorish big spender – I'm glad I'm not anymore.

DRESSLER

We can't all be rich and successful. If everybody was at the top of the heap, there wouldn't be a heap. You don't like the game because you're holding a weak hand at the moment.

EMMETT

I'm not holding any hand.

DRESSLER

Don't worry. As you get older, your dreams will become smaller. They won't even be dreams anymore; just little wishes. "I hope that car over there doesn't splash me," "I pray this cheese hasn't gone off." Little wishes. And some of them will even come true.

MOSS

I'm drunk.

Beat.

EMMETT

(*to DRESSLER*) Have you told him?

MOSS

Told me what?

DRESSLER

Nothing.

EMMETT

Nothing.

DRESSLER

(*to EMMETT*) The opportunity hasn't arisen.

A countdown from above. Cheers. A song. They wash in silence.

Gentlemen, I'd like to propose a toast if I may.

They find glasses with bits of champagne in them.

To the ascendancy of time over all else.

They drink.

What's your resolution?

EMMETT

I'm dispensing with all optimism.

DRESSLER

She hasn't necessarily dumped you for good. She needs to get to know your other qualities.

EMMETT

What would those be?

DRESSLER

Moss?

MOSS

Eh?

DRESSLER

Resolution. It's New Year's.

MOSS

I resolve to hold up my end of things.

He passes out.

DRESSLER

Lovely. And as for myself, I intend to make this my best year, ever, gentlemen. I'm going to do some planting. A little garden; right over there. Grow something from a seed.

EMMETT

Like all those dead plants over there now?

DRESSLER

This year will be different.

EMMETT

How?

DRESSLER

I'm getting one of those growing lights.

EMMETT

And growing what?

DRESSLER

Carrots, I was thinking. That's what life is all about. Cultivating, growing. Gentlemen: to another year.

EMMETT

Another year.

DRESSLER

Cheer up, new guy. There are other fish in the sea.

EMMETT

Well, I'm not looking for a fish.

DRESSLER

I hate to sound trite, but if all she was interested in was your money, then she wasn't really worth it anyway.

EMMETT

I can't believe how shallow people are. Yes, I can. Anyway, she wasn't interested in my money, she has enough of her own. It's the idea that I'm actually working for a living.

DRESSLER

If it's any consolation, you're not doing that great a job here.

EMMETT

Rich people are awful. I'm glad I'm not rich anymore.

DRESSLER

Are you?

EMMETT

Not *glad*, no.

DRESSLER

It's time you stopped thinking about what you were and started thinking about what you are.

EMMETT

Why didn't you tell me about all this?

DRESSLER

All what?

EMMETT

This stuff with Moss. The situation here. I don't want to replace anyone.

DRESSLER

It's unavoidable.

EMMETT

What'll happen to him?

DRESSLER

What happens to us all.

Beat. They look at MOSS; they drink.

Just think how easy it would be to put him out of his misery right now.

EMMETT

Sorry?

DRESSLER

Right now. We could end it all for him. Right here. We could lift his head just ever so slightly toward those smashed potatoes. It would only take a minute. We could say he was drunk when we left for the night; and when we came back in the morning, we found him. Must have fallen over. A tragedy, but a merciful one.

EMMETT

We could, yes.

Beat.

Why would we?

DRESSLER

Don't you ever think about killing someone, just to put them out of their misery.

EMMETT

Only myself.

DRESSLER

What's left; poor sack of shit? No job, no hope, no friends. The rest is suffering, now. Humiliation and suffering.

EMMETT

Yeah, but why should we let him off the hook?

DRESSLER

Right.

They drink, as they look at MOSS. Blackout.

Scene Five

Pipes are dripping. Rain. In the corner, a plant is growing. A coffee break. MOSS sits at one end, smoking; DRESSLER sits at the other, casually looking over the paper.

MOSS
Tell me again?

DRESSLER
They're reviewing your position I think is what I said.

MOSS
That's not what you told me yesterday.

DRESSLER
Didn't I? Well, they're reviewing your position, and once it's been reviewed, then that'll be that. Reviewed.

Flips a page.

Done.

MOSS
What's involved in this reviewing of my position?

DRESSLER
You know the routine; they look over your record and decide. A man fell into a vat of wine.

MOSS
Decide what?

DRESSLER
Eh?

MOSS
Would they fire me? Is that a possibility?

DRESSLER
After such a long, unblemished record of service?

MOSS

I've never missed a day of work.

DRESSLER

Well, exactly. Rather than fire you, they may simply remove your position from the payroll entirely.

MOSS

And then?

DRESSLER

It's not a personal thing. Don't take it personally. It's not you.

Turns another page of the paper.

It's the position.

MOSS

Right.

DRESSLER

You'll just be off the payroll is all.

MOSS

Off the payroll?

DRESSLER

Why speculate at this point?

MOSS

If I'm off the fucking payroll, I'm not employed here.

DRESSLER

One thing doesn't necessarily follow the other.

MOSS

You're full of shit, Dressler.

DRESSLER
Why don't we wait and see. How's your health?

MOSS
Rotten.

DRESSLER
There you are, then.

MOSS
What's that supposed to mean?

DRESSLER
What's what supposed to mean?

MOSS
"There you are, then"?

DRESSLER
I have no idea.

MOSS
You said it.

DRESSLER
Did I? Well, there you are, then.

MOSS
What about him? Why don't they review him?

DRESSLER
He hasn't been here long enough to warrant an assessment.

MOSS
What about you?

DRESSLER
I've had my review.

MOSS

How did it go?

DRESSLER

High marks all around.

MOSS

Congratulations.

DRESSLER

I see your numbers didn't come in again.

EMMETT enters from the bathroom. MOSS moves off, deeply mistrustful of EMMETT. He shows his strength and ability by taking a large garbage can and, with great effort, moving it off. EMMETT comes down to DRESSLER.

EMMETT

Have you told him yet?

DRESSLER

What?

EMMETT

I think you should tell him.

DRESSLER

Not right now. It's not a good time.

EMMETT

When would be a good time?

DRESSLER gives him a look.

I feel – bad for the old goat.

DRESSLER

If you feel bad for him, why would you want me to tell him? If I tell him, it'll break his heart. The trouble is, we live too long, now. People used to drop dead in the middle of their life, and now they hang on until the bitter end. Grasping at every last little opportunity; like drowning men clutching to a raft. Still looking at the want ads?

EMMETT
No.

DRESSLER
Aren't those the want ads?

EMMETT
What? These?

DRESSLER
Ambition. That's what's holding you back.

EMMETT
Ambition is holding me back. I see.

DRESSLER
You could be a great dishwasher if you stopped trying to be something else.

EMMETT
Do you have any idea how much I owe in income tax alone, Dressler? At this rate, I'll be in debt for the rest of my life. Plus there are other people I owe money to, for other reasons. Reasons which – well, I won't go into them right now. But big people, big people with large … fists.

DRESSLER
Why don't you sell that car of yours?

EMMETT
That is the last vestige of sanity in my life. If I start taking the bus at this point, that'll be – public

transit? Anyway, I have another date with my, I guess she would be my ex-fiancée at this point. She's agreed to take another look at the situation. I can't drive her around in a shopping cart.

DRESSLER

This woman's expectations for you are far too high.

EMMETT

They're not high at all. They're just – they're high. But I can reach them again. I can – I can – I just need an entry point. If only I could get back in, I just know I wouldn't make the same mistakes a second time.

DRESSLER

What makes you so sure?

EMMETT

Because I just know. I just – know. This was a painful lesson for me. This is – you don't forget a lesson like this. This is – anyway; there's nothing in here.

Tossing the paper.

Shit jobs. Nothing. I don't need a shit job; I already – well, this isn't a shit job, but it, it, well it doesn't really play to my strengths. You know?

DRESSLER

You're just not applying yourself.

EMMETT

Yeah, I'm not applying myself. I should apply myself. So tell me about this meat thing.

DRESSLER
Meat thing?

EMMETT
Is this something I should know about?

DRESSLER
Know about?

EMMETT
Well, there's perfectly good meat going out the back door here. I'm just – I'm curious.

DRESSLER
Don't be curious.

EMMETT
And yet I am.

DRESSLER
Don't be.

EMMETT
Is this maybe something I could get in on?

DRESSLER
It's really a one-man operation.

EMMETT
OK. But is it maybe something you want me to keep quiet about?

Beat.

Because I can keep quiet about it, if that's the case.

DRESSLER
That's the case.

EMMETT

OK, I was just checking. I'll just keep quiet about it. But, uh, meanwhile, there's a guy I know – and you don't have to answer this right now, but there's this guy and he's sort of a friend, in that kind of way that people sort of think they're your friend, because you did them a favour which wasn't so much a favour as it was a way of getting rid of them, at a time, of course, when you thought you had enough friends, when it turns out you didn't really have any at all, and anyway – he wants me to help him sell this *thing* he's got, and I said, "Gee, I don't think I can because I'd need some place to keep this *thing*, some place safe," and then I thought of the cold storage here. Isn't that funny? I just thought of that right off the top of my head. And with the back entrance here. And, and, and, the thing is, you could be part of this, too. It wouldn't just be a one-man operation as in the case of the meat there. This would be a … be a joint operation.

Beat.

DRESSLER

Are you out of your fucking mind?

EMMETT

What?

DRESSLER

What is this guy? A drug dealer?

EMMETT

A wh – a wh – a – what? Did I say he was a drug dealer? Keep your voice down.

DRESSLER

This is a restaurant. A *restaurant.*

EMMETT

I know that. I'm sorry. I know that.

Beat.

I'm losing my mind, Dressler. I'm actually losing my mind down here. I'm beginning to get used to this; to my room without the window, to my short pants. This morning when I arrived at work, I was whistling. This is not good. I can't get used to this. I can't allow this to be my life. Even if I can't find another job, I think I'm going to have to leave this one.

MOSS

Don't let go of the rope!

EMMETT

What?

DRESSLER

Pay no attention. He's having one of his moments.

MOSS

Hang on, George!

EMMETT

I'm handing in my notice.

DRESSLER

To who?

EMMETT

I don't know. To you?

DRESSLER

Interesting.

EMMETT

Why is it interesting?

DRESSLER

Just when you're making your mark, here. I find that interesting.

EMMETT

Mark? You can't make a mark here. Mark?

DRESSLER

Give it another month.

EMMETT

A month?

DRESSLER

Why not?

EMMETT

It's my spirit. I'm losing that ... irrational and inflated sense of self-worth I used to possess. I'm starting to feel I belong here. And if I belong here, what does that say, Dressler? About me? I'll tell you what it says. I'm not just washing dishes. I'm a *dishwasher*. Which is fine for some, but – it's fine for some. For some.

Beat.

A month.

MOSS

(*from the sink*) Don't stand so close to the edge!

EMMETT sighs, sits at the table, covering his face with his hands, DRESSLER looks up from his paper, impassionate.

End of Act One.

Set of *The Dishwashers* in its premiere production at the Arts Club Theatre in Vancouver, British Columbia.

Set design and photo by Ken MacDonald.

ACT TWO

In a dim, rather moody light, the dishwashers go about their tasks. There is music underscoring the activity, and as the routine builds, it becomes evident that this is a kind of dishwasher dream tango, building in speed and freneticism. The music finishes with a crescendo and the lights return to the drab patina of reality.

Scene One

DRESSLER tends to his carrots. EMMETT sits at the table, composing a letter and smoking.

EMMETT
How's this, then – ?

DRESSLER
We won't be a part of it.

EMMETT
You haven't heard it.

DRESSLER
It goes against our whole philosophy here.

EMMETT
That would be the philosophy, I take it,
of performing menial labour in squalid,

substandard conditions? And by the way, you don't speak for Moss.

DRESSLER

It's doubtful he'll even make it through the treatment.

EMMETT

Why has he decided to have an enema?

DRESSLER

Wasn't a decision; it was a prize. Only thing he's ever won in his life, and it had to be that.

EMMETT

So you don't want to hear this, then?

DRESSLER

Do you know what you're asking these people?

EMMETT

Why do you defend them all the time?

DRESSLER

I can't help it; I believe in this place.

EMMETT

Is that right.

DRESSLER

I love my job.

EMMETT

No you don't.

DRESSLER

It's all I've ever wanted.

EMMETT

With all due respect, Dressler, and I don't mean to be rude, but this isn't a choice; it's a hole we all fell in.

DRESSLER

Every afternoon, when I cross the street, and I peer into the window of this restaurant, it fills me with incredible happiness, I want you to know; to be part of something so beautiful and so elegant. I can see my sparkling white dishes, set out over all the tables. My silverware, lined up like militiamen, to each side. I'm so proud of those god damn little fellas; my forks, my knives, glinting in half-light; my spoons, all at attention; my glassware – those translucent chalices that preside over the tables with such gleaming authority. When people pass by, that's what they see; their very first impression – my handiwork. I was nothing but a prisoner before I came here.

EMMETT

In what sense?

DRESSLER

Federal.

EMMETT

Wow.

Beat.

DRESSLER

You know what happens when we start to make demands? When they can no longer afford our kind of craftsmanship? They go out and they get someone else; someone who doesn't care quite the way we do. And pretty soon the tables are looking a little less respectable. The glasses are cloudy. The cutlery smudged. And the clientele slowly starts to change. Not immediately, but inevitably. Before you know it, chef has quit because the customers are asking for something more *basic*; you know what most people are like. They want food to *eat*, not savour. And one thing leads to another and within a year, this place is doing takeout. Plastic, Styrofoam. That's where it's headed. Down the same path it all goes – down, down – to ordinary town.

EMMETT

Fine. I'll get Moss to sign it. A simple majority is all you need to form a union.

DRESSLER sits to read his paper.

DRESSLER

Two weeks ago, you didn't give a shit about this place; you were ready to bolt.

EMMETT

That was two weeks ago.

DRESSLER

Besides, you build the old man's expectations too high. He's happy with the way things are.

EMMETT

He isn't being paid.

DRESSLER

He doesn't have a job.

EMMETT
There's that.

DRESSLER
He's getting a small sum; I sneak it into his pockets now and again.

EMMETT
You're giving him your own money?

DRESSLER
The restaurant is making an inadvertent donation.

Beat.

EMMETT
You're stealing.

DRESSLER
Not stealing. The spoiled meat we toss out the back –

EMMETT
You mean the meat that isn't spoiled? That spoiled meat?

DRESSLER
I sell it to a man.

EMMETT
A man.

DRESSLER
Who sells it to another man.

EMMETT
Uh, huh.

DRESSLER
He sells it back to the restaurant.

Beat.

It's not the worst crime in this place. I'm not peddling credit card imprints; I'm not siphoning a profit from the soup service, or comping drinks in exchange for large tips. I'm simply removing a product that may or may not at one point go bad; I believe it's called anticipatory spoilage. A common practice in the trade.

EMMETT

How can you justify supporting these people and at the same time stealing from them? Let me see if I can get my head around that. Oh, I can't.

DRESSLER

I'm only doing what they would do if they were better people.

EMMETT

Only, here's the thing: they're not.

DRESSLER

You can't judge them entirely by their behavior towards us. When it comes to caring for a soufflé, you won't find more painstaking attention. They dote like parents over a blanc mange.

EMMETT

You can't be serious.

DRESSLER

It's something.

EMMETT

They're fascists.

DRESSLER
I'll talk to them.

EMMETT
You've talked to them.

DRESSLER
They need a political way out.

EMMETT
These are legitimate grievances.

DRESSLER
This is just a game to you.

EMMETT
No, this is more that just – this is – two weeks ago I was a different man; I wasn't even a man. I was a lost cause. Yes, it's a game. But it's a game we can win. We control this place; you said so yourself. They can't serve food on nothing. Think bigger than yourself for a change. How do you think people succeed in the world?

DRESSLER
You don't need to tell me how people succeed. Running around like fucking jackrabbits, in their fast cars; shouting into phones. They're upstairs right now, eating off my plates. I'd like to kill them all, to be honest. I'd like to stick everyone of them in the eyes with an escargot fork; stab them and stab them repeatedly until their brains gush out through the little holes in their heads. But do I? Why not? Why don't I? I'll tell you. Because my hatred has become my discipline, and my

discipline has become my love. I love this job. Not because it's a good job, but because it's my job. Work. That's all there is. Work, death. The rest is a detour.

EMMETT

I'd like to declare this the most depressing conversation I've ever had.

DRESSLER

Then you haven't cradled your dying old mother in your arms as she prattles on unintelligibly about the child she brought into the world out of contempt for humanity.

EMMETT

No, I haven't.

DRESSLER

Neither have I.

Beat.

Speaking of cars: did you sell that thing yet?

EMMETT

I've put it on the market.

DRESSLER

Good.

EMMETT

Why is that? Why is that good?

DRESSLER

Doesn't suit you anymore. How was your date, anyway?

EMMETT

A total disaster. I told her the truth.

DRESSLER

She would have found out anyway.

EMMETT

She did find out anyway. That's why I told her the truth. It was here in my wrinkled-up hands. There's no mistaking this. Look at this. She took one look at my hands.

DRESSLER

Only honest work could do that.

EMMETT

What makes it honest, Dressler? The fact that we make no money at it? What is it, exactly, this honesty? Is it the filth? The sweat? You think real estate isn't dirty? You think trading in securities doesn't make you sweat? How is a man any more honest because he doesn't take chances? Because he advances not one iota? You know what I think? I think you're a communist at heart; that's what I think. No, wait; not even a communist. At least a communist believes in workers' rights. What are you, Dressler? A guy without dreams; that's all. A guy without dreams. Every man has a right, every woman, every person in this world, every single one of us, has a right to fulfill their dreams. Even you.

DRESSLER

What if they can't?

EMMETT

Can't what? Why can't they?

DRESSLER

(*reading the newspaper*) My stock is doing quite well at the moment.

EMMETT

You have stock?

DRESSLER

No. But I like to keep an eye on it. I would have done quite well.

EMMETT

Why do you put up with this? Because you think you have to. People up there, they don't know we exist. It's time they did.

DRESSLER

You just don't know your place, do you?

EMMETT

I don't have a place. I am my own place.

DRESSLER

When you've lived in this country long enough –

EMMETT

What country?

DRESSLER

– you'll come to realize that there are in fact very few upward opportunities. So you have to look at opportunity as a sideways possibility. Which one of these plates deserves to be picked first? They're all the same. If you were a dish, how would you feel?

EMMETT

A dish?

DRESSLER

Sitting there, waiting your turn.

EMMETT

I don't think a dish sits and waits its turn.

DRESSLER

No; but we do. We all sit and wait our turn; and what if our turn doesn't come? Then what? Do we say it was a waste of time, waiting? Collect our little beatitudes of condolence? It's possible we'll wait our whole lives, and then what? In the end, how do we accept what's become of us if nothing has?

EMMETT

We don't accept.

DRESSLER

Have you watched a man die? I guess not. You know what happens, new guy? He exhales. That's it. The breath goes out, and it doesn't come back in again; and everything he ever was, he isn't anymore. Every hope, every dream, every longing he ever had with every breath, is breathed out of him. My father looked up at me and he said, "Dressler" – he never used my first name; I think he might have forgotten it. "Dressler," he said, "my life has come to nothing." Those were his last words. And I sat there and I thought, well, it's true, but only because he thought it might come to something. He wanted to be a dressmaker, and – well, that's a long story. The point is: ambition is a dream that you wake up from at the very last moment of your life. I don't want to lie on my death bed, wishing, wondering. I want to die with the satisfaction of knowing I accomplished exactly what I set out to – very little; but with the greatest of skill.

DRESSLER turns another page. Blackout.

Scene Two

MOSS smokes through a special device. He is rigged up to a small breathing apparatus. DRESSLER stands, arms folded. They listen to EMMETT.

EMMETT

This is our finest hour, gentlemen. Our chance, should we choose – and we should, not to be too editorial about it – to show what we really are.

MOSS

What are we again?

DRESSLER

Let's just vote and get it over with.

EMMETT

No debate?

DRESSLER

My views are well known.

EMMETT

You seem awfully confident. Has there been some vote-buying? Moss?

DRESSLER

This man, what's left of him, is a man of integrity. A couple of cartons of smokes isn't going to bend his iron will. Moss knows, as we all know, that washing dishes is not an easy job, or a very glamorous one. The only way to make it easier and more glamorous is to replace us with a couple of shiny new machines. We don't want to be replaced with machines, do we Moss?

MOSS answers with a noisy intake of the breathing valve.

EMMETT

This is why we need to organize.

DRESSLER

You say "we," but don't forget: you're new here.

EMMETT

New?

DRESSLER

In terms of seniority, you barely count for half a vote, let alone one. I've been here nearly three decades, and Moss has been here since the beginning of the dishwashing age.

EMMETT

How about if we just stick to the issues? Bad meals, lack of ventilation, ill-fitting uniforms, a paper towel dispenser that doesn't so much dispense towels as *shyly introduce* them.

DRESSLER

Character, it's called.

EMMETT

Let's vote, then.

DRESSLER

Right.

EMMETT hands out the ballots. Music. They vote, as the dumbwaiter shunts more dishes.

EMMETT

Right. Time to count.

DRESSLER

So count.

EMMETT

I'm counting.

He slowly unfolds the first vote.

One "no." A vote for nothing; the status quo. The I-would-rather-die-a-slave-than-change-my-way-of-thinking vote.

DRESSLER

What happens when you lose, by the way? Do you step down from politics altogether, or will you go on a speaking tour?

Another.

EMMETT

One "yes."

DRESSLER

That'll be yours. (*to MOSS*) That'll be his.

The third ballot.

EMMETT

And what's this? Another "yes."

Long beat.

DRESSLER

I'd like to see that.

EMMETT

Scrutinize to your heart's content.

DRESSLER studies the ballot for a long moment. Studies the others. Looks at MOSS.

By my count, that's two "yes"es and one "no." "Yes" takes it by, gosh, a fairly large majority.

DRESSLER

Why'd you do it, Moss?

EMMETT

It's his democratic right.

MOSS

What is?

DRESSLER

Democratic right? You don't have a democratic right. You know what democracy is? A whitewash. Once every four years, your opinion, please; pick one item from this sorry selection. What's democratic about living, I want to know? About some woman walking out on you in the middle of the night, with your entire collection of Strauss waltzes and a gold-plated service pen courtesy of the Knights of Columbus? Democracy is a lazy bitch who never did a day's work in her entire life; then complained if after a late shift, you made too much noise coming home and dropping dead from exhaustion on the sofa. Fuck her! Fuck democracy!

MOSS

You give me no respect.

EMMETT

Not him, Moss.

MOSS

Eh?

EMMETT

Them.

MOSS

Who?

EMMETT

Management. Up there.

MOSS

That's right. Those bastards up there. Some busboy comes up to me the other day, says, "Are you still around?" What the hell is that supposed to mean? Why wouldn't I be around? I'm not just some little ass-scratcher working his way through college. I'm a career man. A full-time employee.

DRESSLER

Employee?

MOSS

Eh?

EMMETT

Nothing. Let's just – don't.

MOSS

I've had enough out of you, Dressler. Stealing my money. Treating me like shit.

DRESSLER

Stealing your money.

MOSS

That's right.

EMMETT

Look, we dishwashers need to stick together here.

DRESSLER

I'd just like to say one thing, Moss. In light of the situation.

MOSS

Go right ahead; say it.

EMMETT

Don't – say it, Dressler; just –

Beat.

DRESSLER

(*to MOSS*) You've done the wrong thing.

MOSS

Oh, I have?

EMMETT

He's voted to move history forward here; that's all.

MOSS

(*privately, to EMMETT*) Three cartons, remember.

DRESSLER

I'll tell you what he's done; what you've both done. You've made a crack in the very foundation of this place.

EMMETT

A couple of nights off and a clean pair of pants that fit isn't going to hurt anyone. Frankly, if this restaurant is so dependent on exploiting people, then maybe it should go under.

DRESSLER
It's what you've thought all along.

EMMETT
What's that?

DRESSLER
You'd rather bring everything down around you than admit what you are; a lowly working stiff.

EMMETT
My God, but you're a sore loser.

DRESSLER
We'll see who loses.

DRESSLER goes to wash dishes.

EMMETT
We've exercised our freedom of expression, Dressler. We're standing up for ourselves.

MOSS
Can we sit down now?

EMMETT
We can do anything we like. Who's going to stop us? We're the dishwashers! The dishwashers!

Beat.

Right.

Beat.

Back to the dishes.

MOSS sits. The lights fade.

Scene Three

MOSS washes dishes.

EMMETT

They're clever. I'll give them that. They agree to everything, and do nothing.

Beat.

You alright?

MOSS

Don't lose your grip.

EMMETT

What?

MOSS

Eh?

EMMETT

Grip?

MOSS

Who?

EMMETT

Let me have that plate. Let go of that.

They struggle with a plate.

MOSS

No!

EMMETT

Listen, Moss. How about some time off?

MOSS

No.

EMMETT

You look –

MOSS

(*grabbing at EMMETT*) Don't let them mention God!

EMMETT

Eh?

MOSS

At the funeral. Don't let anybody mention God.

EMMETT

What funeral?

MOSS

Mine.

EMMETT

Your funeral?

MOSS

That's right.

EMMETT

No God.

MOSS

Not a word.

EMMETT

Why are you talking about a funeral?

Beat.

You've got – years ahead of you. Not years, maybe, but – gosh – days and days.

Beat.

What's wrong with God?

MOSS
You tell me.

EMMETT
Things haven't been that bad.

MOSS
No?

EMMETT
How was the enema?

MOSS
What enema?

EMMETT
Dressler said you won an enema.

MOSS
Don't ever enter a door prize at a medical supply store.

EMMETT
I'll try to remember that. Anyway, let's not talk about funerals and God and all that.

Beat.

I'll do my best.

Beat.

What if there is a God?

MOSS
He has a lot to answer for.

DRESSLER enters from above. Descends. MOSS sits in a pile of potatoes.

DRESSLER
Right. I've been upstairs.

EMMETT
And?

DRESSLER
They're very sympathetic.

EMMETT
Are they.

DRESSLER
Completely on our side.

EMMETT
So you didn't bring it up.

DRESSLER
What?

EMMETT
At all. Didn't bring it up. Anything.

DRESSLER
They're quite familiar with our demands.

EMMETT
And yet no ceiling fan. How is that?

DRESSLER
We have a new towel dispenser.

EMMETT

The front piece just fell off the old one.

DRESSLER

Just as well.

EMMETT

I'm going up there myself.

DRESSLER

There are problems.

EMMETT

What kind of problems?

DRESSLER

Things are not going well this month from a business standpoint. Customers aren't out and about as much in this weather.

EMMETT

It's spring.

DRESSLER

Is it?

EMMETT

If business isn't doing well, then why are we washing just as many dishes as before? It seems to me logical –

DRESSLER

Oh, *logical*! This from a man who studied a language he already knows. But go on.

EMMETT

It seems logical that if there is no appreciable decrease in the number of dishes, then one can *ascertain* –

DRESSLER

Did you hear that, Moss? One can *ascertain.*

EMMETT

– that they're not being completely straightforward with us.

DRESSLER

These people have loftier aims than being straightforward with us. These are restaurateurs. They can't be guided by the normal parameters of managerial conduct.

EMMETT

Apparently they aren't.

DRESSLER

Where's your understanding of the creative process, new guy? You storm in here, manning the barricades, calling for an all out class war, without the least appreciation of the culinary – what's it called.

EMMETT

I don't know. What's it called?

DRESSLER

You talk about this place like it was a business.

EMMETT

Oh, I see. It's not a business.

DRESSLER

It isn't a question of supply and demand. Who's demanding sweetbreads en croute?

MOSS

No one.

DRESSLER

No one; exactly. People need to be led to these things; like slaves to the promised land. You don't go out in search of encrusted headcheese for fuck's sake. Take the case of the artichoke. Only a great mind could have seen its potential – the rest of us would have walked away, thinking "prickly green thing." This is art at its highest level. People don't necessarily want that. They don't really know what they want. They want what they had yesterday: "I want what I had before; that's what I want." Not what's coming tomorrow. But tomorrow, tomorrow is what these people are preparing. It'll be odd, possibly inedible, but it'll be visionary. What'll you be offering us tomorrow, new guy? More whining and complaining? More bitching about workers' rights? Where are you going?

EMMETT

I need some fresh air.

DRESSLER

You're not on a break.

EMMETT

(*rings the break bell*) Oh, look. I'm on a break.

EMMETT heads out.

DRESSLER

You see that, Moss? This is what comes of all these independent ideas. Suddenly people are doing whatever they like. Imagine a world where everyone did whatever they like. You know what I'd like? I'd like to cook my own hands and eat them. How about that?

MOSS

I'd like to fly.

DRESSLER

Where?

MOSS

Around.

EMMETT returns for his cigarettes.

DRESSLER

This is a war. You don't have democracy in a war, new guy.

EMMETT

What war?

DRESSLER

What war, he says! What war! Did you hear that? The war of principled conduct. *Grace*, stupid. Excellence in the food services. We're fighting against the tide. The *tide.*

EMMETT

Oh. Did you hear that? That was the sound of me not caring anymore. Suddenly, something in my head went "pop"; like that. Pop. Hear it? Pop. I quit. See. I quit. Quit, quit, quit, quit. Quit. The inflated balloon of my own stupidity; burst suddenly. I've had enough. I'd be surprised if you even presented them with our list of grievances in the first place.

The possibility occurs to him. He marches over and opens DRESSLER's locker. The list falls out. Beat.

DRESSLER

You would have been out of a job.

EMMETT
Right.

DRESSLER
Besides, Moss didn't even know what he was agreeing to. Did you, Moss?

MOSS
Eh?

DRESSLER
He was acting on impulse. Being swayed by the crowd.

MOSS
I was bribed!

DRESSLER
Look at him. He would have been the first to go. I don't say he's my responsibility, but I couldn't see the poor idiot chucked out into the alley like yesterday's scraps. It's not like that here. They look after their own here.

EMMETT
Then why did they fire him?

Beat.

I don't mean fire, Moss, I mean –

MOSS
What?

EMMETT
Nothing.

MOSS
I've been fired?

DRESSLER
No.

MOSS
Why would they fire me?

DRESSLER
They wouldn't.

EMMETT
That's the trouble. They would. They did and you might as well know it. Do you think they give a shit about a decrepit, smelly old man, with one lung and a tortoise? They're impervious. How do I know? Because I was one of them. Business doesn't operate any other way.

Beat.

MOSS
I'm a dishwasher here.

DRESSLER
You are.

MOSS
I've always held up my end of things.

DRESSLER
You have.

MOSS
When it comes to it, when it comes right down to it, they can always say that. "Moss held up his end." Can't they say that? I've held up my end here. I have.

DRESSLER
You don't, anymore. You don't, Moss.

Beat.

The truth of it is this: if you were any slower, time itself would start moving backwards.

MOSS
I've never left a dish unwashed.

EMMETT
What does that matter to them? You're just part of the machine.

MOSS
I never let down the operation.

DRESSLER
You do, now.

EMMETT
Sorry I, uh – sorry, Moss.

Beat.

MOSS
It's true, then.

DRESSLER
Yes.

EMMETT
It's true.

MOSS walks away to the dishes. Starts furiously scrubbing a pan.

DRESSLER
Why did you have to tell him? Why?

EMMETT
It was an accident.

DRESSLER
You're the accident.

EMMETT
Moss?

DRESSLER
That pan is clean, Moss.

MOSS drops the pan. Stands motionless.

EMMETT
Is he alright?

DRESSLER
Moss?

MOSS
George?

DRESSLER
It's us, Moss. Us. There's no George. That's before our time.

MOSS
I have to let go, now.

DRESSLER
Don't let go.

EMMETT
What's he talking about?

DRESSLER
I have no idea. Moss. What are you talking about?

MOSS
Sorry.

MOSS walks a little toward the stair.

Sorry.

He stops; disoriented.

EMMETT

Would you like to sit down?

MOSS

I'd like to sit down.

EMMETT goes for a chair.

DRESSLER

Take it easy, Moss.

MOSS

Eh?

DRESSLER

Nobody wants anybody dropping dead down here.

MOSS drops dead. Blackout.

Scene Four

DRESSLER finds a receptacle for the cremation ashes. EMMETT folds up the old man's apron.

DRESSLER

The sun came out this morning, did you notice?

Beat.

EMMETT

You weren't supposed to mention God, by the way.

DRESSLER

Why not?

EMMETT

I told you. He didn't want any mention of God. He was very specific about it.

DRESSLER

Who's to know? Two impatient-looking men from the crematorium, and a woman waiting for a bus.

EMMETT

It was his only request.

DRESSLER

What did you think of the rest of the eulogy?

EMMETT

Where did you get all that information?

DRESSLER

Off the top of my head.

EMMETT

He wasn't in the navy?

DRESSLER

I was.

EMMETT

Were you?

DRESSLER

Not the navy, no.

EMMETT

Do we even have a navy?

DRESSLER

It was actually a – more of a – ferry, really; I worked in the kitchen.

EMMETT
Do you know *anything* about Moss?

DRESSLER
Before he washed dishes he washed cars. Before he washed cars, he washed windows.

EMMETT
His life had a bit of a theme, then.

DRESSLER
Not all of us can say that.

EMMETT
Are you looking at me?

DRESSLER
Not at all.

EMMETT
What was it about washing, I wonder?

DRESSLER
Not hard to say. It's the starting over. The clean sweep of things. Whoosh.

EMMETT
Mm.

DRESSLER
Like a soul after confession.

EMMETT
Soul?

DRESSLER
If you confess your sins, your soul is wiped clean.

EMMETT

You mean if I went out and killed someone with my bare hands, and I came back and told you about it, blood all over me, my soul would be clean again?

DRESSLER

Something like that.

EMMETT

Stupidest thing I ever heard.

DRESSLER

Why?

EMMETT

A soul is not a thing. So you can't wipe it clean.

DRESSLER

How do you know it's not a thing?

EMMETT

That's a medical fact; so you can't wipe it clean. And anyway, even speaking metaphorically –

DRESSLER

Oh, metaphorically.

EMMETT

– you can't just drop your sins off at the laundry; you absorb them into your being. If you're going to compare the soul to anything – a futile exercise if ever there was one – at least compare it to a … bouillabaisse. Or tofu.

DRESSLER

Is there any champagne in the buspans?

DRESSLER gets a couple of glasses and some leftover champagne from a buspan. EMMETT is inconsolable. DRESSLER pours, then hands out drinks, then toasts.

He always held up his end. Until he couldn't anymore.

They both drink.

EMMETT

I'm going, by the way. I've done my time here.

DRESSLER

I thought you'd given up on that idea.

EMMETT

Why would you think that?

DRESSLER

I was under the impression –

EMMETT

Uh, huh.

DRESSLER

– that since you were still here, you had no intention of – you know –

EMMETT

Right.

DRESSLER

– leaving. After all the effort you've put into making changes. You've had an impact, I want you to know. Perhaps not an impact, so much as a – what's it called when a stone hits the –

EMMETT

Water?

DRESSLER

You can't expect a ceiling fan overnight.

EMMETT

I have a future to think of.

DRESSLER

A future.

EMMETT

You know? That thing that some people have in front of them instead of, I don't know, dishes?

DRESSLER goes back to work.

I'm not going anywhere.

DRESSLER

I thought you said you were.

EMMETT

I just saw the whole thing. Right there in front of me. Just now. Like a hopeless riddle. The present *is* the future. I'm going to be doing this for the rest of my life.

Beat.

I have nothing. All I ever had to begin with was gumption, and I don't even have that anymore.

DRESSLER

You have some dishwashing experience.

EMMETT

I have some dishwashing experience; true.

DRESSLER

Why not make the best of it?

EMMETT

Best of what? What's the best of it? Getting the burnt sugar out of a saucepan?

DRESSLER

There's more to it than that.

EMMETT

I'm sorry; you're right. There's roasted duck grease, and caramelized baby leaks. There's lime oil and balsamic reduction. There's puree and and buerre monte and glaze. There's a sea of wet sludge and I'm drowning in it.

DRESSLER picks up EMMETT's gloves, walks over and beats him with them.

DRESSLER

You have to pull yourself together here.

EMMETT returns to work.

EMMETT

I'll die in a pile of potatoes. I'm more important than this. I know I am.

DRESSLER

Are you.

EMMETT

Not hugely I don't mean, but relatively? And I don't mean to say this isn't important on some level – some very … unimportant –

DRESSLER

It isn't *what* you do in life.

EMMETT

Oh. Really. Is that – ? Oh, good. Because I thought it was. I thought it mattered what you did. I guess I was under some false impression. You see, I thought all along that washing dishes was completely meaningless, because no matter how well you clean them, they all come back dirty again.

DRESSLER hands back a plate.

DRESSLER

You missed a spot.

EMMETT

Did I?

EMMETT scrubs, harder and harder, then smashes the plate to the ground.

There. How's that?

He smashes plates, one after another, as the lights fade to black.

Scene Five

Later. DRESSLER works, stopping once or twice to look in the direction of the washroom. In a moment, EMMETT appears from the washroom, dressed in his civvies. DRESSLER works some more; stops when he notices EMMETT looking at him.

DRESSLER

I realize it can be discouraging down here, at times. But I want you to know that it doesn't go unnoticed. When all is said and done, they appreciate our efforts.

EMMETT

I know it's what you believe, Dressler. But has anyone ever come down here and said as much?

DRESSLER

It's what you don't understand about people. Their well-meaningness, their gratitude, sometimes, just has to be assumed. It's called "supposition of accountability."

EMMETT

Have you had a word with them at least?

DRESSLER

A what?

EMMETT

At least? A word with them?

Beat.

You can't do this job by yourself.

DRESSLER

What are you suggesting?

EMMETT

I'll go talk to them. This is –

DRESSLER

No.

EMMETT

I've got nothing to lose.

DRESSLER

I don't want them thinking there are problems down here. They'll find someone.

EMMETT

It could be weeks, months.

DRESSLER

I've never in my life caused a problem. Understand?

EMMETT

Why not?

DRESSLER

BECAUSE. I'M. A. PROFESSIONAL!!

Beat.

EMMETT

Of course you are.

DRESSLER

Leave it as it is. Leave it just as it is. Everything.

Beat.

How did the exam go?

EMMETT

There was a question about spoons and forks.

DRESSLER

No kidding.

EMMETT

A math question, but with spoons and forks. I thought that was interesting.

DRESSLER

Did you?

EMMETT

Not really, no.

DRESSLER
Well, let's hope she's impressed with your efforts.

EMMETT
I'm not doing it for her. Did I say I was doing it for her?

DRESSLER
You don't seem the legal type, if I may say so.

EMMETT
The law part, OK, that was her idea.

DRESSLER
I hope it all works out.

EMMETT
Thank you, Dressler.

DRESSLER
I never had a son, as you know.

EMMETT
Gee, well – you hardly think of me as a –

DRESSLER
Eh?

EMMETT
A son.

DRESSLER
Son?

EMMETT
But that's –

DRESSLER
I was talking about my testicle.

EMMETT
Ah.

DRESSLER
I find after all this time, I still miss it.

EMMETT
I'm sorry. Are you – comparing me to a testicle? I don't –

DRESSLER
No. I was talking about attachment. Things you become attached to, even when they're no longer attached.

EMMETT
Right.

DRESSLER
You may find that you miss this place is what I'm saying.

EMMETT
Uh, huh.

DRESSLER
Don't get too caught up in that. Move on. Not everybody can be a dishwasher.

EMMETT
I was a dishwasher.

DRESSLER
You were – never – you were never a dishwasher.

EMMETT
What do you mean?

DRESSLER

You couldn't hack it. (*tapping his forehead*) Up here.

EMMETT

It's not much of a challenge up here. I think that was a major part of the, uh, the, uh –

DRESSLER

Uh, huh.

EMMETT

Nothing to gain.

DRESSLER

What's there to gain, new guy? Eh? Why do people carry on at all? Do you ever wonder? People, every day, just going about their lives? Do you ever wonder?

EMMETT

I do wonder.

Beat.

DRESSLER

I'd like to draw your attention, if I may, to this spider web, over here.

EMMETT

What spider web?

DRESSLER

Exactly. Did you know that every night for a month now, when we lock up and leave, a spider makes a web from here to here; a beautiful, perfect web? And every morning, when I come in to work, I walk right through it. But every night, she comes back again, and weaves another one. She must sit there all day, planning that web. She must spend all night making the damn thing. Is she stupid, or is she smart?

EMMETT

She's a spider.

DRESSLER

Tell her that.

EMMETT

I can't – tell her that.

DRESSLER

Excuse me.

DRESSLER goes back to his newspaper. He stops for a moment. Takes a deep breath. Continues. EMMETT starts to leave.

EMMETT

I don't feel bad about leaving here. Not one bit.

DRESSLER

Good.

EMMETT

It is good. It's very good. Goodbye, Dressler.

DRESSLER

A dog fell twelve storeys and lived.

EMMETT

It isn't really that I don't have a commitment to this place. It's more like I don't really have a commitment to any place. Is that – ? Is that – ?

DRESSLER

What an interesting commentary on life.

EMMETT

Do you think so?

DRESSLER

Eh?

EMMETT

You think … you think maybe there's something out of order in the world, now. That we have … that we have nothing, anymore; no ideas, no reasons, just naked self-interest and cold ambition?

DRESSLER

What are you talking about?

EMMETT

I don't know. What are you talking about?

DRESSLER

Moss's numbers here.

EMMETT

What? His lottery numbers?

DRESSLER

They came through.

EMMETT

They did?

DRESSLER

Not all of them, no. But a couple.

Beat.

Trust; you've just got to have trust, see.

EMMETT

Trust; right.

DRESSLER

And a little patience.

Beat. EMMETT escapes up the stairs; the door closes. DRESSLER looks up for a moment, then goes back to his newspaper. Blackout.

Scene Six

DRESSLER sits with his paper, daydreaming, eating a carrot. He turns the page. A young man enters from the bathroom in dirty, ill-fitting whites. This is BURROUGHS. He looks at the dishes as DRESSLER looks at him. DRESSLER stands, goes over to the boy, and puts an arm around his shoulder.

DRESSLER

Perfect fit.

BURROUGHS

Don't you think these sleeves are a little – ?

DRESSLER

No. What?

BURROUGHS

– short?

DRESSLER

Are they? Now you don't have to roll them up.

BURROUGHS
Have you got another – ?

DRESSLER
No. If I may, I'd like to draw your attention over here to the sink. This is where you'll be spending most of your time.

BURROUGHS
Yeah?

DRESSLER
I hope you're up for this.

BURROUGHS
I'm up for it.

DRESSLER
You know what this is?

BURROUGHS
An elevator of some kind?

DRESSLER
Not an elevator of some kind, an elevator of a very special kind. This is what brings us the dirty dishes; this is what takes the clean dishes away. What happens in between is entirely up to us. Got that?

BURROUGHS
Yeah. I got it.

DRESSLER
Do you?

BURROUGHS
Yeah.

DRESSLER

I want you to imagine for a minute this restaurant without any clean dishes. It's a frightening thought. Chaos. Right? Maybe you're young, and hey, the idea of anarchy is still attractive to you, but that'll change, over time. I'm telling you; you'll come to know what order means. You won't clean dishes because you have to anymore, you'll clean dishes because you want to. Got that?

BURROUGHS

I think so.

DRESSLER

So what's your name?

BURROUGHS

Burroughs. But you can call me Eddie.

DRESSLER

I'm not calling you anything, pal. You don't have a name down here until you earn one. Got that? We don't just hand that sort of thing out. We had a guy down here once, worked for two years almost – never once used his name. Not once. So what do you think of that?

BURROUGHS

Harsh.

DRESSLER

You bet it is. Pick that plate up.

BURROUGHS

This one?

DRESSLER

Yeah. Pick it up. Look at it.

BURROUGHS
OK.

DRESSLER
Have a good look. What do you see?

BURROUGHS
Gunk.

DRESSLER
Look beyond the gunk.

BURROUGHS
I don't –

DRESSLER
You know what I see? Don't waste my time guessing, I'll tell you. Duty. Duty is what I see. We've all got one in life; and if we don't have one, we better get one. Am I right?

BURROUGHS
I guess.

DRESSLER
Don't guess. What are your interests? By and large.

BURROUGHS
I'm a drummer.

DRESSLER
Oh, yeah? With what?

BURROUGHS
Drums?

DRESSLER
I mean with an orchestra or what?

BURROUGHS
I'm looking for a band.

DRESSLER
Do I care? This is the hot sprayer. See what happens?

BURROUGHS
It sprays.

DRESSLER
Don't say it like that. This isn't just spraying. This is our advance work. See this? Look. Meringue! You might as well give up right now if that gets past you. That reconstitutes itself in the hot wash – you got yourself a meltdown! Look at this. Know what that is? Big wedding tonight. I hate weddings. The same god damn dinner on every plate. This one's the bride's. Not a bite out of it. See?

BURROUGHS
What's this?

DRESSLER
Someone always loses a speech.

BURROUGHS
Should we send it back up?

DRESSLER
Don't ever tamper with fate.

The door above flies open; from the kitchen we hear EMMETT.

EMMETT
It's alright. It's OK. I know my way around.

Now EMMETT appears at the top of the stairs, dressed in a tuxedo.

Dressler! Dressler!

He descends, stopping at the bottom.

How are you, Dressler? How are you?

DRESSLER
Fine, thank you.

EMMETT
It's me, Dressler. Me! Emmett!

DRESSLER
Is that right?

EMMETT
That's right. Me.

DRESSLER
Right. I didn't see it at first.

EMMETT
Sorry about the outfit. I got married tonight. Married the woman of my dreams. Can you believe it? Anyway, it fits. Look at that! Like a glove. The pants; look – all the way down to the ankle.

DRESSLER
You're right. It fits. You look very –

EMMETT
I know.

DRESSLER
– successful.

EMMETT

I do, don't I? Things have turned around pretty quickly, I've got to tell you. I climbed those stairs, Dressler, and I haven't stop climbing.

DRESSLER

So you married the rich girl; it all worked out.

EMMETT

Don't say it like that. Sure she's rich, but don't say it like that. It all worked out, yeah. It all worked out. She had a change of heart. A change of heart.

DRESSLER

Really?

EMMETT

Not really, no. *Really*, she doesn't have a heart. Forgive me. I've had a bit to drink. I'm not usually this – whatever the word is. But yes; congratulate me. I have now met all her husband criteria. "Not a dishwasher" was the real clincher. Yeah, what do you know. Suddenly, I'm material for advancement up the, up the – who's this? The new guy? Hello, new guy.

BURROUGHS

Sir.

EMMETT

He called me sir.

DRESSLER

If you'll excuse us, we've got a lot of work piling up here.

EMMETT

Sure. Sure; don't let me stop you. Don't let me stand in the way of – of this important – this commendable work.

DRESSLER

As a rule, we don't fraternize with the customers. It's not the policy of the restaurant to let people in, behind the scenes. There's a certain magic that we do, that's spoiled, if you know what I mean, by seeing the mechanics of the thing.

EMMETT

I just, I felt the need –

DRESSLER

Did you?

EMMETT

– to come and, yeah –

DRESSLER

Uh, huh.

EMMETT

Just – yes, tell you what a marvelous job you're doing down here. It really is beautiful, you know. The sparkling china, the glittering silverware; everything lined up so smartly. People don't know what you do. They just stuff food into their faces. They're pigs, Dressler. You were right. They'll never stop being pigs. It frightens me, frankly. If I were you, I wouldn't wash another dish for the gluttons of this world. They mock you with their appetites. And yet, here you are.

DRESSLER

Here I am.

EMMETT

I just wanted to tell you. Someone up there appreciates you. See? I wanted you to know that your faith has not been completely wasted.

DRESSLER

It wasn't necessary.

EMMETT

Make sure those plates don't touch each other, new guy.

BURROUGHS

No, sir.

EMMETT

No, sir. A finger width; is that right?

DRESSLER

Why did you choose this restaurant? I find it interesting.

EMMETT

Me? Are you kidding? She does all the choosing.

DRESSLER

Really? And knowing you used to work here.

EMMETT

Well, exactly.

EMMETT wanders over to the table and sits.

That's her subtle way, Dressler. Let's have our wedding reception in the restaurant where

Emmett used to wash dishes. She likes to put things in perspective that way.

Beat.

But I'm happy, I have to say. On the whole, I'd have to say, taken altogether – everything. My life is coming back into focus; I'm getting it back together. The law thing, well, that didn't – but I'm involved in the investment side of the business. They've got a lot of holdings, the family, and it's like a fish in water for me. I breathe that stuff, you know? It's like I have gills. I think her father is very impressed. It's hard to tell, because he never smiles, but he's, he's okay. He's a prick, but he's –

DRESSLER
Maybe you should go back up and join them.

EMMETT
You're right. What am I doing down here? I don't belong here. Of course, I don't belong up there, either; but I definitely don't belong down here.

DRESSLER
Go back to your wife.

EMMETT
I'm going to – excuse me; I'm going to go back to my wife.

Beat. He stops.

This was the best job I ever had. No it wasn't; it was the worst job. But, no, it was the best.

DRESSLER
You really have had a bit to drink.

EMMETT

I have. Haven't I? Have I? I have. But in a way, I'm sober, too. Perhaps I have reached the pinnacle of my soberness. Perhaps I have realized, in this moment of nearly hallucinogenic clarity, that washing dishes is the ideal occupation; water pressure is about the only pressure down here.

Getting up, he stumbles across the room and suddenly rushes to the sink, grabbing a plate and the sprayer and spraying wildly.

I just – here! Give me that!

DRESSLER

What are you doing? Stop that. *Stop – it.*

EMMETT

I want my job back!

They fight over the hose until DRESSLER retrieves it. EMMETT has drenched himself.

DRESSLER

Get out.

EMMETT

Excuse me, gentlemen. I apologize for interrupting your work. I just wanted to say that I'm on my way, now. And I'm going places. But I'll never forget my roots. Well, no; I'll forget my roots. I'll forget. I'll move over the landscape above you, and never ever think of you again. Why? Because a person needs to forget, that there are crap jobs, and slime under every rock, and grease, grease, with no end. And – I can't remember the rest. But, but Dressler – that moment between us. What happened to that moment? When you were supposed to look over at me and say my name. Remember? "Hey, Emmett." I worked my ass off down here.

DRESSLER
And then you gave up.

EMMETT
Fuck you. Sorry.

Long beat.

Sorry.

Beat.

Fuck you. OK. Goodnight. I'm on my way. Hey; new guy. What's your name?

BURROUGHS
Burroughs, sir.

EMMETT
That's right. Don't ever accept your fate, Burroughs. Don't ever accept your fate.

BURROUGHS
No, sir.

EMMETT
No. Sir.

EMMETT staggers up and out.

DRESSLER
Immigrant. Worked his way up in the world. Doesn't happen often; almost never at all. You got that?

BURROUGHS
Yeah, I got it.

DRESSLER

Do you? Good. Let it be a warning.

BURROUGHS

OK.

Beat.

How?

DRESSLER

You think you're a big shot?

BURROUGHS

I'm not.

DRESSLER

You're not.

BURROUGHS

I know.

DRESSLER

You're not.

BURROUGHS

That's what I said.

DRESSLER

OK. Because you see this pile of dishes here? It's bigger than both of us.

BURROUGHS

Yeah.

DRESSLER

Yeah. You know what else? Always will be.

Beat. They return to work. As the lights fade the sound of the restaurant above – dishes, patrons – grows louder and louder.

Blackout. The End.